The Culture of the

ISLAMIC WORLD

Vic Kovacs

PowerKiDS
press™

New York

Published in 2017 by **The Rosen Publishing Group, Inc.**
29 East 21st Street, New York, NY 10010

Cataloging-in-Publication Data

Names: Kovacs, Vic.
Title: The culture of the Islamic World / Vic Kovacs.
Description: New York : PowerKids Press, 2017. | Series: Ancient cultures and civilizations | Includes index.
Identifiers: ISBN 9781499422580 (pbk.) | ISBN 9781499422597 (library bound) | ISBN 9781508151524 (6 pack)
Subjects: LCSH: Islamic civilization--Juvenile literature. | Islamic Empire--Juvenile literature.
Classification: LCC DS38.3 K68 2017 | DDC 909.0976701--dc23

Developed and produced for Rosen by BlueAppleWorks Inc.

Art Director: Haley Harasymiw
Managing Editor for BlueAppleWorks: Melissa McClellan
Editors: Janice Dyer, Marcia Abramson
Design: T.J. Choleva

Picture credits: p. 5 Otto Pilny/Public Domain; p. 7 Eugène Fromentin/Public Domain; p. 9 Jean-Joseph
Benjamin-Constant/Public Domain; p. 11 inset Bertl123/Shutterstock; p. 11 Konstantin Kapıdağlı/Public
Domain; p.12 Juan de la Corte/Public Domain; p. 15 William Logsdail/Public Domain; p. 17 Léon Belly/Public
Domain; p. 18, 18 inset Edwin Lord Weeks/Public Domain; p. 21 Seqoya/Shutterstock; p. 21 inset Mikhail
Markovskiy/Shutterstock; p. 22 liquid studios/Shutterstock; p. 22 inset Anilah/Shutterstock; p. 23 Waj/
Shutterstock; p. 24 kyoshida0710/Shutterstock; p. 24 inset Philip Lange/Shutterstock; p. 25 Nikita Maykov/
Shutterstock; p. 27 August Querfurt/Public Domain; p. 28 Zurijeta/Shutterstock; p. 29 Fedor Selivanov/
Shutterstock; Maps: p. 5 inset T.J. Choleva / Shutterstock: Anton Balazh; p. 6 T.J. Choleva/Shutterstock: adike;
p. 10 T.J. Choleva/Shutterstock: Mclek adike

Manufactured in the United States of America
CPSIA Compliance Information: Batch #BS16PK: For Further Information contact Rosen Publishing, New York, New York at 1-800-237-9932

CONTENTS

CHAPTER 1

THE BIRTH OF ISLAM

The beginnings of Islam are traced to A.D. 610, in the city of Mecca. In this year, the Prophet Muhammad said he started having visions and hearing voices that were sent from God, or Allah. Based on these signs, Muhammad began building a **religion** and attracting followers. These followers came to be known as Muslims. Many there did not agree with his idea that there was only one God. The tribes in Mecca were mostly **polytheists**, which means they believed in many gods. As a result of this disagreement, Muhammad and his followers soon moved to the nearby city of Medina. This **immigration**, which took place in the year 622, is also the start of the Islamic calendar.

In Medina, Muhammad established an Islamic state, the first of its kind. This state and its laws were based on the teachings found in the Quran, the Islamic **holy** book. Eight years later, Muhammad returned to Mecca and **converted** the entire city to Islam. Today, Mecca is the most holy site in the world for Muslims.

ISLAM AND MUSLIMS

The word "Islam" comes from the Arabic word "salema," which means peace, purity, and obedience. The Islamic religion teaches followers to obey the will of God and His law. Followers of Islam are called Muslims, which means "one who submits (to God)."

After the city of Mecca converted to Islam, other tribes and cities in the area converted as well. By the time Muhammad died, the entire Arabian peninsula was Islamic.

Arabian
Peninsula
Medina
Mecca

THE SPREAD OF ISLAM

After Muhammad's death in A.D. 633, Islam, entered a long period of expansion. Muslim armies began spreading Islam throughout the Middle East. Next, the armies conquered North Africa, including Egypt. Then the Muslim Arabs invaded Europe. The area known today as Spain came under Muslim control in 711. However, the Muslim armies were defeated in the Battle of Tours in 733, which took place in the area known today as France. This battle stopped the rest of Europe from falling under Muslim rule. However, Islam remained powerful in the southwest corner of Europe (Spain, Portugal, and Andorra) until the fifteenth century.

The **Byzantine Empire** in the East also helped prevent the Muslim takeover of Europe. Muslim forces managed to defeat the Byzantine presence in Egypt, but the empire stood firm until 1453, when it was finally defeated by **Sultan** Mehmed II.

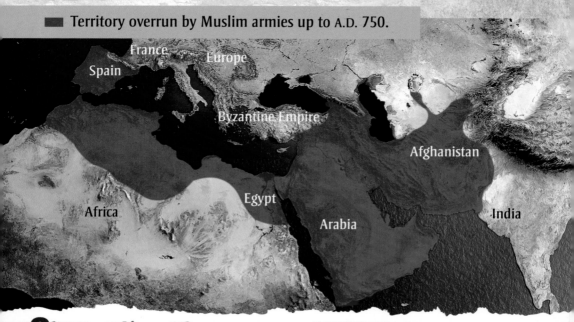

Territory overrun by Muslim armies up to A.D. 750.

France
Europe
Spain
Byzantine Empire
Afghanistan
Egypt
Africa
Arabia
India

Islam brought together individual tribes in Arabia. These tribes joined together to become large armies that conquered large areas.

Although the early Muslim armies were prevented from spreading Islam further into Europe, Islam's rule grew at an incredible speed in a short time. In the 100 years after the birth of the religion, Islam spread west from Arabia to Spain and east to Afghanistan. Wars between the Christian and the Islamic faiths marked the course of history.

Muslim armies were very powerful. Together with **diplomacy**, an increase in trade, and the expansion of the later Ottoman Empire, Islam kept spreading further and further. Over time, Islam spread to the Atlantic Ocean in the east, to South and East Asia, and all the way to the Pacific Ocean. The Muslim Mughal Empire ruled over large parts of India and Afghanistan, and Islamic culture thrived in many locations in Malaysia, Indonesia, and China.

CHAPTER 2

THE OTTOMAN EMPIRE

The Ottoman Empire first emerged around the turn of the fourteenth century. Starting in Anatolia, where modern Turkey is today, it eventually became one of the largest and most powerful empires in the world. Its reign lasted all the way until the twentieth century, ending only in 1922, after World War I. Islam was the official religion of the empire.

The empire was founded by in 1299 by Osman I, who was the leader of a tribe of Islamic Turkish warriors. During Osman's reign, the empire conquered its first Byzantine cities in Anatolia. The conflict between the Islamic Ottoman Empire and the Christian Byzantine Empire reached a turning point in 1453. That was the year the Byzantine capital, Constantinople, finally fell to the Ottomans.

Although the Byzantine Empire drove off earlier Muslim invasions, by 1453 the empire was not what it once was. Facing a 50-day siege from Sultan Mehmed II, Constantinople could only raise 10,000 men to defend it. With a force at least ten times bigger than that, the Muslim Turks easily took the city. With this defeat, the Byzantine Empire was no more. Mehmed changed the city's name to Istanbul, and declared it the new capital of the Ottoman Empire. The city was well positioned to allow Muslims to advance farther into Europe.

After he captured Constantinople, Sultan Mehmed II conquered territories in Anatolia and the Balkans. These areas formed the Ottoman Empire's heartland for the next four centuries.

9

The empire went on to conquer large parts of Europe, Asia, and Africa. During the sixteenth and seventeenth centuries, at the height of its power under the rule of Suleiman the Magnificent, the Ottoman Empire controlled Western Asia, the Caucasus, North Africa, the Horn of Africa, and much of Southeast Europe. European territories included Greece, Bulgaria, Romania, and Hungary. Ottoman armies went as far as Vienna in present-day Austria, where their European conquests were halted for good by their defeat in 1683.

LEADERSHIP AND SOCIAL CLASSES

The leaders of the Ottoman Empire were called sultans. The sultan possessed absolute power over the affairs of the empire. He was in charge of all the state's affairs, including matters related to the government, the military, and religion. Sultans answered only to Allah, and lived according to God's Law, called Sharia.

■ Ottoman Empire at its height

Europe

Vienna

Southeast
Europe

Caucasus

Greece

Western Asia

Asia

North Africa

Africa

Horn of Africa

The sultan and his court lived in Topkapi Palace, a large palace in present-day Turkey. As many as 4,000 people lived in the palace. The activities in the palace followed strict rules.

Below the sultan was the divan, a council of advisers that was led by the grand vizier. This council debated and discussed matters of the empire. The grand vizier's duty was to inform the sultan of the opinions offered during these meetings. The sultan was then free to act on this advice, or ignore it.

Because the empire was so large, the sultan could not be everywhere at once to make every decision. Territories had leaders called beys, who served as governors. Beys worked with qadis, who were administrators for smaller towns or rural areas.

There were four main social classes in the Ottoman Empire. The men of the pen were the top class, and included judges, lawyers, imams, doctors, and other educated people.

Next were the men of the sword, who were members of the military. After that were the men of negotiation, who were mostly merchants. Lastly were the men of husbandry, who were farmers, shepherds, and the like.

MIGHTY MILITARY POWER

For most of its reign, the Ottoman Empire was based on a series of reforms made by Mehmed II during his rule. Gunpowder started to be used around this time, and the Ottomans put it to good use. This new technology allowed them to use cannons that helped to destroy the walls of Constantinople, leading to its fall.

The Ottoman army consisted of three parts: the **infantry**, the **cavalry**, and the **artillery**. The infantry was made up of foot soldiers. One elite branch of the infantry was called the Janissaries.

The Ottomans had a large navy. Their ships held cannons, which were useful in sinking enemy ships.

THE TRUE DRACULA

One notable opponent of the Ottoman Empire was Vlad III. Vlad was the prince of Wallachia, a region of Romania. His father, Vlad II, had been a member of an order of Christian knights, the Order of the Dragon. Their mission was to stop Ottoman invasions into Christian Europe. It was from this order that the elder Vlad gained one of his names, Vlad Dracul, meaning Vlad the Dragon. Vlad III, his son, was called the Son of Dracul, or Vlad Dracula in the Romanian language.

As a child, Vlad III was held hostage by the Ottoman Empire. Though he was educated and treated relatively well as a captive, Vlad always resented being held against his will.

After his release, Vlad began fighting the Ottomans. As prince of Wallachia, he became famous for his brutality against his enemies. He was well known for **impaling** his opponents on spikes, a practice that gave him another fearful name, Vlad the Impaler. Not only was impalement a terrible way to die, but it served as a form of **psychological warfare**. For example, during one particular retreat, Vlad Dracula left thousands of Ottoman soldiers impaled and dying in a field as a warning to their **allies** that were coming after him.

Local peasants who witnessed Vlad Dracula's horrific methods started spreading the often overblown tales of Dracula's cruelty and lust for blood. The bloodthirsty vampire legend was born.

Made up of enslaved Christian boys taken from Ottoman territories, Janissaries were trained from a very young age. Since they were paid a salary and were always on call, they are today considered the first modern standing army. The cavalry, also called the sipahi, was made up of some of the most skillful horsemen in the world. The artillery division was responsible for the cannons that helped make the Ottoman army so feared.

CHAPTER 4

LIFE IN THE ISLAMIC WORLD

Life in the Islamic world was centered around religion. The Quran and the teachings of the prophet Muhammad were the basis for all things. These included laws and the justice system, the pursuit of knowledge, and even family affairs. It also influenced how people interacted with non-Muslims. Non-Muslims included other members of Islamic society, or foreigners that Muslims traded with.

THE FAITH OF THE PROPHET

Islam is a **monotheistic** religion. This means that its members believe that there is only one God, who is called Allah. The Quran is a holy book, similar to the Christian Bible, that Muslims believe is the exact word of Allah. The founder of the religion, the prophet Muhammad, is also honored. He is considered the last prophet of God.

Prayer is very important in Islam, with five prayers required throughout the day. These prayers are called Salat. Another major aspect of Islam is Ramadan, the ninth month of the Islamic calendar. During this month, Muslims don't eat or drink anything between sunrise and sunset. This practice is called fasting. Ramadan ends with the holiday of Eid al-Fitr.

Muslims are expected to give money to charity. They pay a special tax to their community once each year to help poorer Muslims.

The Quran tells men and women to dress modestly. In some countries, women must cover their head or face in public.

15

Muslims are expected to complete the journey to the holy city of Mecca, or the Hajj, at least once in their lives. This type of journey is called a **pilgrimage**. In 2015, over 1.3 million foreign Muslims visited the city. Mecca is very important in Islam. The prophet Muhammad and the religion of Islam were both born in the city. During Salat, all prayers are done in the direction of Mecca. It is so important that when a Muslim dies, they are often buried with their face turned toward Mecca.

LIFE OF THE DHIMMI

The dhimmi were non-Muslims living in Islamic lands. These included Christians and Jews, as well as Hindus and Buddhists in India. In Arabic, the word dhimmi means protected person. They paid a tax called the jizyah, which was different from the zakat that Muslims paid. The jizyah was somewhat stricter than the zakat, and was based on the total wealth of the taxpayer. The zakat was based on how much the taxpayer had left over after reaching a certain amount of wealth.

Occasionally, more than just money was taken. The devşirme was a practice in the Ottoman Empire when Ottoman soldiers were sent to collect Christian boys from the villages in Ottoman territories.

PEOPLE OF THE BOOK

Jews and Christians were the original dhimmi. Islam respects the teachings of Abraham, who is the founder of monotheistic religion in all three faiths, as described in their holy scriptures. Because of these similarities, Muslims considered Jews and Christians fellow People of the Book.

During medieval times, tens of thousands of pilgrims would gather in big cities. They would then travel to Mecca in caravans.

Boys from Christian families between the ages of 8 and 18 were taken from their homes, brought to Istanbul, and converted to Islam. They were then trained to serve the empire, either in the military or as government workers. Although the most gifted boys could achieve high status in the empire, the practice was not popular and was stopped in 1648.

For the most part, dhimmi were treated fairly well for conquered people. They were allowed to hold their own courts, according to their own religious laws, if their dispute was with someone of the same faith. If not, they were tried in Islamic courts. They were also permitted to do certain things that were forbidden to Muslims, like eat pork and drink alcohol. Jews in particular often experienced less persecution under Muslim rule than they might have in Christian territories.

While dhimmi were allowed to practice their own religion, they were not allowed to display religious icons like crucifixes on the outside of buildings, or on clothes. Churches could not be built, or even repaired, without permission. Failure to pay the jizyah tax could have drastic effects. If the status of dhimmi was taken away, a person could be enslaved, or even killed. As a general rule, however, dhimmi were treated decently.

MUSLIM TRADERS

Islamic trade routes stretched from the Middle East to Europe, China, and North Africa. Longer land routes usually used camels to transport goods, whereas sea routes used boats. Spices were a popular item to import from the Far East into Islamic lands. It wasn't just goods that were traded between the early Islamic Empire and the rest of the world.

Merchants carried most of their goods on camels that moved in large caravans over great distances.

SLAVES IN ISLAMIC SOCIETIES

Throughout history, Islamic societies have used slaves. Many worked as various kinds of servants, including cooks. The Ottoman Empire actually had slaves all the way up to the early twentieth century. However, slaves were able to become extremely important members of the empire. Children taken as part of the devşirme were a type of slave, but they often went on to become important members of the military. They also held high positions in politics and as administrators. Domestic servants existed in the empire, but were much less common than warrior slaves.

Islam itself was a popular export. Many of the cultures that Muslims encountered ended up converting to Islam. Knowledge was also spread through trade. Once translated into Latin, many of the works of Muslim scholars were widely read throughout Europe. Trading routes first established by Muslims remained in use for hundreds of years.

FAMILY LIFE

In the Islamic world, men have typically been the head of the family. Traditionally, men were allowed up to four wives, as long as they could afford them and cared for them. Women were only allowed one husband. In most Muslim societies, the home has been the woman's domain. Men were responsible for supporting the family financially. In Islam, it's believed that spiritually, both men and women are equals and were created to complement one another. As a result, they were both given different, but equally important skills and tasks. Of course, customs varied based on location and era.

CHAPTER 3

ISLAMIC ARCHITECTURE AND SCIENCES

Islamic architecture is almost as old as the faith itself. As the religion grew and spread, its followers began building **mosques**, **minarets**, and other structures. The earliest of these grew out of earlier architectural traditions. In time, though, they would come to express a uniquely Muslim style.

MOSQUES AND PALACES

Throughout history, the mosque has been the most important building in Islamic life. A place of worship, similar to a Christian church or Jewish synagogue, mosques were often huge buildings, built to welcome many worshippers.

As Islam spread to new areas, its architecture included the styles traditionally found in these regions. These influences include Byzantine, Persian, and Roman architecture. One particular feature that was initially borrowed from Christian architecture was domes. However, over time, domes came to be associated with Muslim buildings.

THE DOME OF THE ROCK

The Dome of the Rock was first built in A.D. 691. Located in Jerusalem, it is built on a plateau that is holy to Muslims, as well as Jews. In Islam, it is believed to be where Muhammad ascended to Heaven. It still stands today, and is the oldest example of Muslim architecture that remains on Earth.

The historic Sultan Ahmed Mosque in Istanbul combines some Byzantine features, such as domes, with traditional Islamic architecture.

Tall, slim towers called minarets were another typical feature of mosques. Built taller than the rest of a mosque, minarets provided a visual focal point, and were used to call the local population to prayers. Another common feature of the Islamic style was horseshoe-shaped arches. **Mosaics** were popular decorations.

Palaces were also prominent in the Muslim world. These grand structures were typically home to important figures in the Islamic world. They usually had private areas, including living quarters, and public spaces, like meeting halls, reception rooms, and large open courts. Though many of them were similar to mosques, they also varied greatly based on where and when they were built. One example is the Alhambra, a fortress with a large palace inside its walls.

The famous fortress complex Alhambra in Spain became a Christian palace in 1492. At that time, Spanish monarchs Ferdinand and Isabela conquered the city of Granada from Muslims.

THE TAJ MAHAL

Possibly the most famous Islamic building is the Taj Mahal. The Taj Mahal was built by Shah Jahan, an emperor of the Muslim Mughal Empire. The building was constructed to hold the **tomb** of Mumtaz Mahal, his favorite wife. Finished in 1648, it took 20,000 skilled workers to build the Taj Mahal.

The building is made of white marble with beautiful carvings and decorations on inside and outside walls. At its center is the tomb, a grand domed building surrounded by four minarets. A large pool that reflects the image of the building is set among lush gardens and fountains.

Known as "the jewel of Muslim art in India," the Taj Mahal draws about three million visitors a year.

Built in Granada on the Iberian Peninsula, it is a great example of Moorish architecture. Because of its distance from the main Islamic centers, it has some common Islamic features, like domes and horseshoe-shaped arches, but it is missing others.

ISLAMIC ART

Islam discourages showing living figures in art. This grew out of a law forbidding showing images of Allah, the prophet Muhammad, or his relatives. This has grown to include all living beings believed to have been created by Allah. As a result, much of the art that developed in Islam showed more abstract, geometrical designs.

The arabesque is considered to be both art and science. The designs are mathematically precise, while at the same time beautiful and symbolic.

Floral or vine motifs were often used to decorate the walls and ceilings of mosques. They are known as arabesques. Another popular Muslim art form was calligraphy. This was because it was thought that to write Allah's words from the Quran in a beautiful way was to give Him glory.

EDUCATION AND CULTURE

Education has always been important in Muslim society. In the Ottoman Empire, primary schools were established that welcomed all Muslim children, both girls and boys, beginning at age five. They learned reading and writing, and received religious instruction.

The state ran the palace school, which trained both the princes of the sultan, as well as Christian children who were forcibly taken from their homes and converted to Islam under the devşirme rule. Christian children joined a branch of the palace school called the enderun school. There, they were trained to become bureaucrats, government workers, or soldiers. The highly gifted were taken to Topkapi Palace in Istanbul, where their education continued.

Because of its belief in education, Islamic society contributed many great scientific minds to the world. Great works of scholarship in Greek, Latin, and Chinese were translated into Arabic, and were built upon by Islamic scholars. The Golden Age of Islamic science is generally thought to be between the eighth and thirteenth centuries, when major advancements were made in various fields. In medicine, the study of diseases and surgery were greatly improved. The **Canon** of Medicine, a medical encyclopedia written by Avicenna, was published in 1025. It remained one of the most important medical texts in use for hundreds of years. Other subjects that were advanced by Muslims during the Golden Age were mathematics, astronomy, and chemistry.

Avicenna was one of the most important thinkers and writers from the Islamic Golden Age. He wrote 450 works on a variety of topics, including philosophy, medicine, astronomy, mathematics, and geology.

CHAPTER 5

TOWARD MODERN TIMES

During the Golden Age of the Islamic Empire, a series of **caliphates** spread the religion and conquered many territories. This was a period of great intellectual progress. After Baghdad fell to Mongol invaders in 1258, Islam lost its biggest city, and the Golden Age ended. However, the Ottoman Empire emerged as a major power in the fourteenth century, and became a successor to the previous caliphates. At the height of its power, in the seventeenth century, it held territory in three continents: Africa, Asia, and Europe. Eventually, this empire would also fall into decline. Many historians point to a lack of good leadership from the later sultans as a major reason for this fall.

By the twentieth century, the empire had shrunk considerably. It was at war almost non-stop during its last years. After entering World War I in the Middle East, the empire eventually surrendered to Allied forces. The Allies' attempts to partition the empire directly led to the Turkish War of Independence. This war led to the founding of modern-day Turkey. It also led to the expulsion of the sultan and his family from the country for 50 years, and officially ended the Ottoman Empire.

The battle of Vienna in 1683 stopped the advance of the Ottoman Empire into Europe. Over the sixteen years following the battle, southern Hungary and Transylvania were largely cleared of the Turkish forces. A slow but steady decline of the Ottoman Empire followed.

27

Today, there are no longer huge Muslim empires. However, there are independent Muslim countries. Pakistan was formed as a country for Indian Muslims in 1947. Iran became an Islamic republic in 1979. Other countries, like Saudi Arabia, have Islamic monarchies, meaning they are ruled by a Muslim royal family. These countries are some of the most powerful in the world, showing that Islam still continues to affect modern affairs.

More than half of the world's Muslims today live in South and Southeast Asia. Indonesia, India, Bangladesh, and Pakistan have the largest Muslim populations. Immigration has helped spread Islam all around the world. It can be found in China, England, and the United States. Islam is the second largest religion on earth, with 1.6 billion members. The only religion with more followers is Christianity.

The Kaaba is a building in the middle of a sacred mosque in Mecca. It is called the "House of God." Muslims around the world face the Kaaba during their daily prayers. Muslim pilgrims gather in the Kaaba during the Hajj.

Today's Saudi Arabia was the birthplace of Islam. It is the world's largest oil producer and the oil industry makes up most of its economy.

The modern world is still affected by developments made during the Golden Age of the Islamic Empire. Their advancements in astronomy, medicine, and mathematics are being studied to this day. They also helped to preserve much of the knowledge that came before them, from ancient cultures like the Greeks and the Romans.

When much of Europe was overtaken by the **Dark Ages**, Islam helped to keep important works of great minds safe, as well as building on their ideas. They even established some of the world's first libraries. Society would be a very different place today without the contributions of the Muslim world.

GLOSSARY

allies: nations that fight together and support each other

artillery: a branch of the military that uses mounted weapons

Byzantine Empire: a society based in modern-day Greece

caliphate: a type of Islamic government that emerged after the death of the prophet Muhammad

canon: an officially accepted body of knowledge

cavalry: a branch of the military trained to fight on horseback

convert: to cause someone to change to a different religion

Dark Ages: the period in European history from about A.D. 476 to about A.D. 1000

diplomacy: negotiating using peaceful means

holy: having spiritual importance

immigration: the movement of people to one particular country

impale: to pierce through a body with a sharp stick or stake

infantry: foot soldiers, soldiers who fight on the ground

minaret: tall towers that are part of a mosque and used to call the population to prayers

monotheist: someone who believes that there is only one God

mosaic: a picture made of small pieces of stone, tile, or glass

mosque: a place of worship for Muslims

pilgrimage: a journey to a place of spiritual importance

polytheist: someone who believes in many gods, not just one

psychological warfare: the use of threats and terror to threaten and scare one's enemy

religion: a collection of spiritual ideas, rituals, and customs that provides a way to live one's life

sultan: the leader of the Ottoman Empire, similar to a king

tomb: a building made specifically to hold the bodies of the dead

FOR MORE INFORMATION

Books

Barnard, Bryn. *The Genius of Islam: How Muslims Made the Modern World.* New York, NY: Knopf Books for Young Readers, 2011.

D'oyen, Fatima M. *Islamic Manners Activity Book.* Markfield, UK: Kube, 2012

National Geographic. *1001 Inventions and Awesome Facts from Muslim Civilization.* Des Moines, IA: National Geographic Children's Books, 2012.

Websites

Due to the changing nature of Internet links, PowerKids Press has developed an online list of websites related to the subject of this book. This site is updated regularly. Please use this link to access the list:

www.powerkidslinks.com/acc/islam

INDEX